The Comanche Perspective

A New Lens on the Council House Fight

by

DAVIS TRUMAN

2 .... *The Comanche Perspective*

Davis Truman© Copyright 2024 - All rights reserved.

The content contained within this book may not be reproduced, duplicated, or transmitted without direct written permission from the author or the publisher.

Under no circumstances will any blame or legal responsibility be held against the publisher or author for any damages, reparation, or monetary loss due to the information contained within this book. Either directly or indirectly.

Legal Notice:

This book is copyright-protected. This book is only for personal use. You cannot amend, distribute, sell, use, quote, or paraphrase any part of the content within this book without the author's or publisher's consent.

Disclaimer Notice:

Please note the information contained within this document is for educational and entertainment purposes only. All effort has been executed to present accurate, up-to-date, and reliable, complete information. No warranties of any kind are declared or implied. Readers acknowledge that the author does not render legal, financial, medical, or professional advice. The content within this book has been derived from various sources. Please consult a licensed professional before attempting any techniques outlined in this book.

By reading this document, the reader agrees that under no circumstances is the author responsible for any losses, direct or indirect, which are incurred as a result of the use of the information contained within this document, including, but not limited to, — errors, omissions, or inaccuracies.

4 .... *The Comanche Perspective*

Table of Contents

CHAPTER ONE 8

INTRODUCTION 8

CHAPTERTWO 25

COMANCHE RELATIONS 25

CHAPTER THREE 42

THE RISE OF VIOLENCE 42

CHAPTER FOUR 59

THE PRACTICE OF CAPTIVE 59

CHAPTER FIVE 79

THE COUNCIL HOUSE FIGHT 79

CHAPTER SIX 99

THE CLASH 99

CHAPTER SEVEN 109

A BIG MISTAKE 109

CHAPTER EIGHT 124

.... *The Comanche Perspective*

THE AFTERMATH OF THE COUNCIL HOUSE FIGHT 124

Davis Truman ....

CHAPTER ONE

INTRODUCTION

The Republic of Texas in the 1840s was the setting for intermittent warfare between the Texians and the Indians who resided within the country. As settlements grew and more land was required, increased contact and resistance from the Indians of Texas resulted. The greatest of these threats to white settlement were the Comanche warriors. Many attempts to create peace and frontier stability failed because most Texians were unwilling to share their land, and the Mirabeau B. Lamar administration declared war on the native population. The Council House Fight was one influential Battle within the larger untraditional war between the Euroamerican settlers and the native populations that troubled the Republic. For years, the Indians have been blamed for what occurred in San Antonio on March 19, 1840, citing past difficulties and deceptions on the part of the Penateka Comanches that were present that day.

But the Texians were also guilty in their dealings with the Comanches. This thesis will argue that neither the Texians nor Indians were without blame, and both shared responsibility for the deterioration of events on and before March 19, 1840. Years before the Americans came to dominate the region, the Spanish in the eighteenth and early nineteenth centuries, and the Mexicans beginning in 1821, had difficulty dealing with the natives, especially the Comanche. The

Lipan Apache were the first major threat to the Spanish colonization of Texas, but they were quickly replaced by a more fierce opponent. As the more dominant nomadic group, the Comanche moved further south, lured by European goods and horses, and pushed the Apache closer to Spanish settlements. Eventually, unable to sustain the constant raids of the Comanche bands, the Apache of the San Antonio region reached out to Spanish officials for protection in the form of a mission and a presidio. Established in 1757, the Mission Santa Cruz de San Saba was destroyed by Comanche attacks and was never rebuilt. Motivated by the necessity for peace in the region, the Spanish sought negotiations with many of the Comanche bands, and peace treaties were signed in October 1785.

Peace lasted for much of the Spanish rule in Texas and remained mutually beneficial for both groups, granting Comanche access to European goods and the Spanish security on the frontier. The intrusion of illegal traders from the United States in Texas caused renewed difficulties in the region because they traded guns and ammunition to the Comanche. Angry with the Spanish for failing to maintain their promises in the treaty of 1785, the Comanche began a series of raids against the settlements of San Antonio in 1818. In response to an official inquiry based upon the complaints made by one of the members of the Bexar ayuntamiento, an army officer, Juan Antonio Padilla, submitted a report calling the Comanche "treacherous, revengeful, sly, untrustworthy, ferocious, and cruel, when victorious; cowardly and low, when conquered," and claimed they were "inconsistent in their friendships and break their contracts for any cause."

Despite the relative peace enjoyed throughout Texas, the Spanish lost control of the region to Mexican revolutionaries in 1821. Independent Mexico sought to strengthen its defenses against the presence of illegal American entrepreneurs and Indian attacks on the frontier. Their first step toward achieving this goal was to allow Stephen F. Austin to bring three hundred American families to settle in Mexican Texas. The Mexicans hoped to create a "nucleus of Roman Catholics" to help curb American expansionist efforts inside Texas.

The early Texian leadership did not want war and initially wanted to coexist peacefully. However, repeated Indian attacks angered many of the colonists, and the people's demands for retaliatory raids were too strong for men like Austin. Though the Comanche would become the Texians' most fearsome and dangerous enemies, it was mostly the Karankawas and the Tonkawas, Wacos, and Tawakonis that troubled the first American settlers. During this time of great demand to stop the Indians from continuing their raids against the Texians, Austin organized the first group of Texas Rangers to defend the frontier settlements.

In June of 1822, a schooner, the Only Son, arrived in Texas with one of the first groups of Austin's colonists. When the immigrants moved inland, the Karankawas attacked and killed the guards and took the supplies still aboard the ship. This became a pattern for the early Texas colonists: the Indians would attack when they found whites alone or in small groups. Though Austin preferred peace, the conflict between the

Karankawas and the colonists made that impossible. It was not only the memory of these early interactions with the Indians of Texas but later colonists' own experiences within and outside the settlements for years to come that helped create fear and hatred for the natives in the mindsets of the Texians.

Indian depredations continued to plague the area, and in 1823, Mexico concluded a peace treaty with the Comanche Indians in which they promised to stop the raids committed by their young warriors in return for increased trade. As the opportunity for trade lagged, internal divisions led some Penateka Comanche bands to seek continued peace with the Mexicans, while others chose to conduct raids into Mexican settlements. As the Texian revolutionary threat grew inside the province, the Mexicans shifted their focus to that threat. Although the American settlers attempted to enlist the Indians of Texas against the Mexicans, few joined their revolutionary efforts, and the Comanches played no military role for either side.

Conflict between the Texians and the Indians continued after Texas won its independence. The American settlers who formed most of the new populace of the Republic of Texas were mostly from other southern states and had experience dealing with Indians. In fact, some of the Indians that now occupied Texas had been forced there and away from their traditional homelands in other parts of North America years earlier by Americans pushing frontier settlement westward. Like their predecessors, the Texians sought ways to deal with their Indian problem. During his first term as president of the Republic of Texas, Sam Houston dealt with the Indians differently than most Texians wished, and he sought treaties and other more peaceful solutions. But after the election of Lamar, who began a war of extermination, conditions worsened inside the Republic. Lamar had developed his hatred for Indians early in his career under the tutelage of Georgia Governor George M. Troup, whom he had served as a private secretary. In Georgia, there had been a bitter struggle between the state and the federal government concerning the removal of the Creek and Cherokee Indians from lands that they had rightfully claimed. A treaty had been signed at Indian Springs and ratified by the Senate, but it quickly became controversial when the majority of the Creek nation began to renounce its signing. President John Quincy Adams investigated the Creek's claims and "found the treaty had been obtained by fraud, refused to proclaim it in effect, and ordered that new negotiations should be begun."

Angered, Lamar organized the Georgia militia to resist Adams' demands, and this experience left a bad taste in Lamar's mouth for the Indians. Lamar's first opportunity to initiate his Indian policy began with the Cherokee in East Texas. The Cherokee had come to Texas around 1824, under the leadership of Chief Bowles, and settled on land highly desired by many white settlers coming to the territory.

Following the Texas Revolution, Texians remained concerned about a potential alliance between Mexicans and Native American tribes, particularly the Cherokee. These fears intensified in 1837 when Cherokee and Mexican officials met in Matamoros, reinforcing suspicions of collaboration. President Lamar, influenced by his experiences in the Georgia Creek Wars, believed that Native Americans should obey the laws of the Republic if they were to remain. As evidence of a Cherokee-Mexican alliance emerged, Lamar viewed it as treasonous and demanded that the Cherokee leave Texas. In response to these concerns, the Texian Congress passed legislation in December 1838 to protect the northern and western frontiers by building a military road and establishing forts. Additionally, they called for a regiment and mounted volunteers to defend the Republic against potential threats from the Cherokee's connections with Mexico.

President Mirabeau B. Lamar's plan to expel the Cherokee from Texas aligned with the anti-Indian policies of Secretary of War General Albert Sidney Johnston and Commissioner of Indian Affairs George W. Bonnell. Lamar informed the Cherokee that the Republic of Texas would not tolerate their involvement in the Cordova Rebellion and alleged treason. Chief Bowles, the Cherokee leader, acknowledged that peaceful coexistence with white settlers was unlikely and requested compensation for their improvements on the land they were to leave. Although Lamar agreed to compensate them, he warned that force would be used if they did not depart peacefully. Despite efforts to negotiate a peaceful exit, conflict erupted, and by Christmas Day 1839, the Cherokee were forcibly removed to Indian Territory.

The expulsion of the Cherokee was driven by Texian fears of their alliance with Mexico and a desire for more land in Texas, which was occupied by the Cherokee. Many Texians were unwilling to coexist with Native Americans. With the Cherokee removed, the Comanche became the primary Native American threat to the Texians, continuing to raid settlements, take captives, and demand ransoms. Past attempts at peace with the Comanche had consistently failed.

The Comanche, like many nomadic Native American tribes, were composed of several independent groups with distinct customs. This diversity made it difficult for the Texians to understand their social structure, leading to misunderstandings during negotiations. Treaties with one Comanche band did not apply to others, and the continued raids on Texian settlements, combined with the Texians' lack of understanding, led to the conclusion that coexistence was impossible. As a result, the Texians saw war as the only solution to deal with the Comanche, whom they viewed as enemies of the Republic.

The Comanche, in turn, were both apprehensive and defiant in their dealings with the Texians. They were angered by ongoing Texian raids, as well as by American encroachments on their traditional hunting grounds. Unfair treaties further eroded their land, leading many Comanche to resist further negotiations. A significant example of this encroachment was the establishment of Austin in 1839, which overlooked Comanche hunting grounds along the Colorado River. As Texian settlement expanded in this region, tensions between the settlers and the Comanche escalated.

While some Comanche groups could coexist with the Texians, most struggled to negotiate lasting treaties that satisfied both sides. The interactions between the Texians and Native Americans, particularly the Penateka Comanche, were marked by numerous skirmishes, battles, and mutual atrocities. The Council House Fight in 1840 was a notable example of these tragic conflicts during the pre-statehood years in Texas. In early January 1840, a small group of Comanche approached San Antonio to negotiate a lasting peace with the Texians. They agreed to release all American captives and return with a larger delegation to finalize the peace terms. However, the Texians, mistrustful of the Comanche's intentions, sent troops to San Antonio. On March 19, 1840, when sixty-five Comanche arrived, they brought only one American captive, Matilda Lockhart, who was in poor condition and revealed that the Comanche planned to ransom the remaining captives one by one. Enraged by what they saw as another broken promise, the Texians detained the twelve principal Comanche chiefs inside San Antonio's Council House, demanding the release of all captives. When the chiefs denied the accusations, tensions escalated, leading to a violent confrontation as one Chief attempted to escape.

Within minutes of the initial confrontation, all twelve Comanche chiefs were killed, and the violence quickly spread to the streets of San Antonio. By the end of the day, thirty-five Comanche and seven Texians were dead, with many other Comanche captured and imprisoned. The heavy loss of life, particularly among the Comanche, has led to lingering questions about the true nature of the event. With limited primary documentation, interpretations vary. Some argue that the Comanche were at fault for misleading the Texians about releasing their captives, while others blame the Texians for detaining and killing men who had come under a flag of peace. The reality is more complex, with both sides responsible for the tragic outcome.

The mutual misunderstandings, cultural ignorance, and entrenched hostility between the Texians and the Penateka Comanche had created a situation where peaceful resolution was no longer possible, culminating in the Council House Fight.

CHAPTER TWO
COMANCHE RELATIONS

The Americans who came to Texas encountered many hardships on the frontier. The central threat and barrier to their settlement was the native people of the region, especially the Comanche. The Comanche Indians dominated the southern plains and are still the most well-recognized of the Indian tribes of Texas today. The Comanche, or Nermernuh, was a hunter-gatherer society originally composed of the Northern Shoshone people from the mountains of Wyoming. Their lives were revolutionized in the late seventeenth century when they acquired horses from the Spanish. They eventually migrated south and were the last indigenous group to arrive in Texas around 1700. The first documented evidence of the Comanche's arrival in Texas is dated 1743, when they appeared in the Spanish settlement of San Antonio in search of their enemies, the Lipan Apaches. Unlike other groups, the Comanche did not descend upon the plains in one unified body; they traveled in many different family groups at different times. Despite their lack of unity, the Comanche's entrance into the region drove out other natives, such as some Jumano, Pueblo, and Apache people.

The Comanche remained a nomadic people whose range extended from the Red River area to northern Mexico. Once established in Texas, they hunted buffalo, which provided them food, clothing, and shelter. The Comanche, a powerful society, soon dominated the southern plains and much of its commerce. As a result, Americans and Comanches developed a trade network long before Anglo colonization. Still, as these same American settlers permanently encroached upon their hunting grounds, their relationships deteriorated. The Comanches comprised different independent divisions, bands, and families. At one time, there were over a dozen Comanche bands, varying in size, the territory they occupied, and in some cultural respects.

In Comanche culture, it is taboo to say the name of a deceased relative. Therefore, group names evolved, making listing or tracing the many different bands in Comanche's history nearly impossible. According to the Comanche Nation of today, there may have been as many as thirty-five groups simultaneously. Still, in the nineteenth century, there were five clearly identified Comanche bands. These include the Penatuka, or "Honey Eaters Band," also referred to as the "Quick Striking Band"; the Yapaituka, or "Root Eaters Band"; the Noyuka, or "Wanderers Band"; the Kwaharu, or "Antelope Eaters Band"; and the Kuutsutuka, the "Buffalo Eaters Band."

Because of the unique nature of the Comanche organization, attempts to create peace treaties often failed. Democratic principles were deeply embedded in Comanche's political organization. Each tribal division or band had two chiefs, a civil or peace chief and a war chief. The position of civil Chief was largely advisory, for he lacked the power to compel obedience. These positions were not hierarchical, and band members chose who would lead by community consent. Chiefs retained their authority as long as they could maintain the confidence of their band members, and leadership positions often passed within the same powerful families. The individual Comanche remained free to do as he wished, which contributed to the weakness of civil or peace chiefs as war leaders evolved into civil headmen as Indian–white violence grew. The societal structure was not rigid; bands coalesced and broke apart depending on the needs and goals of the members. Their rather loose social organization allowed individuals to cross not only between bands but divisions as well. When one band of the Comanche signed a peace treaty, it in no way bound other bands to its promises. Further complicating peace negotiations was that leaders elected to represent the Comanche divisions to American authorities were considered intermediaries with limited influence.

The power granted them by their people gave these "chiefs" no influence or authority beyond a specific diplomatic context. But while some were only "spokesmen," many were political leaders of local and larger social and political groups. American, Spanish, and Mexican officials had difficulty understanding the different cultural practices and often misunderstood the Comanche organization, making trying to work together difficult. Working with the Comanche remained complicated but not impossible for some groups. Spanish Indian policy initially encouraged peace and stability in their territories and punished raids and killings as well. But as frontier violence continued, the Spanish "encouraged warfare between Indian nations as a means of breaking their power."

The ensuing cycle of violence and times of relative peace directly influenced the development and growth of the Spanish settlement at San Antonio de Bexar, beginning in 1716. Developed as a paramilitary settlement, San Antonio de Bexar's citizens were situated in the center of hostile Indian territory and were compensated for their willingness to occupy such dangerous territory for the Spanish crown. San Antonio was developed in isolation far north of other Spanish colonies and was meant to serve as a buffer from European and Indian encroachment.

As the French threat in East Texas grew in 1719, Bexar was reinforced until, eventually, five missions inhabited by Coahuiltecan Indians thrived in the vicinity, protected by the local presidio from their enemies, the Apache, Comanche, and other Norteno groups. The first hostilities the citizens of San Antonio encountered were the

Lipan Apache in the 1720s. The Apache usually raided for horses, and because their enemies, the Comanche, were encroaching upon their territory, the Apaches wanted access to the European goods they had been accustomed to and were now cut off from in New Mexico. The Spanish had difficulty dealing with these natives because, unlike the Spanish social structure, the Apache and Comanche, as well as other nomadic Indians, were not one united people but a group of independent bands or people. As the Spanish concluded peace treaties with one group, another continued to raid their settlements. Rural property, livestock, and lone ranch hands were always at risk, and outlying ranches were largely abandoned.

Agriculture based on crops and livestock faced problems expanding beyond the immediate vicinity of San Antonio due to these constant threats that also forestalled the development of formal, well-organized estates or haciendas. As a result, Spanish officials renewed their efforts to make peace with the Indians. Eventually, the Apache received a mission and a presidio to help protect them from Comanche and Nortenos. For decades, Tonkawas, Yojuanes, Bidais, Karankawas, Yrripiames, and others had sought Spanish protection, and the new alliance between the Spanish and the Apache angered these groups. To these natives, the Spanish became their new enemy, and war was declared against them.

In 1757, the Spanish completed the Santa Cruz de San Saba mission for the Lipan Apache. Angered at their new alliance, the Comanche attacked the mission on March 16, 1757. They stole horses and goods, killed cattle and oxen and eight people, and set fire to buildings they had already looted. Those who were not decapitated, scalped, or otherwise brutalized made their way to the presidio, where they safely waited out the assault. The mission of Santa Cruz de San Saba was the only Texas mission destroyed by an Indian attack and was never rebuilt. When conditions worsened as violence increased, the Spanish changed their policy. For the remainder of the eighteenth century, the Spanish would make friends with the Apache's enemies and wage war on the Apache, as well as conclude treaties with other groups like the Comanche and encourage them to fight the Apache as well.

Spanish-Indian policy was thus always changing for their different needs, and it was never simple. In the summer of 1785, the Spanish sent emissaries out among the Comanches, inviting them to a peace conference at San Antonio de Bexar. Three chieftains accepted, and a treaty was signed with the Eastern Comanche in October 1785. Many promises were made to one another, as this end to hostilities was to extend to all Spanish settlements beyond Texas borders. The Comanche pledged to ransom or return all Spanish captives, not allow foreigners into their villages, and continue their war on the Apache Indians.

Both the Comanche and Spaniards assured each other that friends and enemies of both parties would remain their friends and enemies. And last but not least, the Spanish promised to present the Comanche with annual gifts. Because this peace was mutually beneficial, it lasted for the next thirty years. The Comanche loved their annual gifts that demonstrated their authority, and eventually, the Indians were given muskets, powder, and shots. As a result, the Spanish overlooked the occasional raids made by the Comanche in Texas. They even bought captives from México that the Comanche brought to San Antonio de Bexar for ransom. The Spanish-controlled Texas settlement of San Antonio de Bexar experienced many difficulties. Still, it firmly established itself as a place for future engagements, both violent and diplomatic, with the Indians of Texas. The Comanche remained at peace with the Spanish for the remainder of their rule in Texas, but it hinged on the fact that the Spanish provided them with gifts, profitable trade, and waged war on their shared enemies, the Apache.

Eventually, a treaty was signed with the Western Comanche in 1786. However, confusion still existed, and Spanish officials appealed to the Indians to appoint one leader to represent their entire tribe in future affairs.

Ecueracapa stepped up to the challenge, but his limited time of united leadership ended with his death in 1793. The Spanish presence in Texas was minimal, and most of their relationship with the Comanche was based on mutually beneficial trade. The Comanche would help keep the Americans out as enemies of Spain, and in return, they would receive highly desired luxury items like metal goods and, more importantly, the horse. The Spanish looked at the natives as a buffer between their settlements and the United States and welcomed their residence within the territory overall.

As trade increased between the Spanish and the Comanche, so did the Comanche's desire to obtain more goods, especially guns. Eventually, some guns were traded between the Spanish and the Comanche, but when they could not get what they wanted from the

Spaniards, the Comanche turned to illegal American traders. For example, Cordero, a prominent Penateka Comanche leader, was on good terms with American traders and Indian agents in Natchitoches, Louisiana, who had given him a military uniform, a sword, and a letter attesting to his friendship with the United States. Such items were visible signs of the Chief's power and increased Cordero's prestige among his people. Americans provided guns, metal implements, beads, cloth, vermillion, and even arrowheads in exchange for buffalo robes and furs, as well as stolen mules and horses from Spanish-controlled Mexico.

Many of these illegal American traders on the South Canadian and Red Rivers also encouraged raids on Spanish outposts. This alliance complicated Spanish-American relations, which were already hostile, and -

relations between the Spanish and Comanche, who had been bound by treaty to keep one another's friends and enemies.

As a result of Comanche's trade with the Americans, the Spanish bought their own American goods. They employed Samuel Davenport to run a trading post at Nacogdoches to counteract the influence of illegal American traders in the region. The Spanish new policy had some success, as Cordero and other Comanche became dependent on trade with Davenport. But a shift away from trade with the Spanish accelerated after 1812 when an American filibustering expedition to overthrow Spanish authority, led by Augustus W. Magee and Jose Bernardo Gutierrez de Lara, captured Nacogdoches, Goliad, and San Antonio. Eventually, they were defeated on the Medina River in 1813, but this embarrassment to the

Spanish only demonstrated their weakness and confirmed that American interest in Texas was growing. Throughout Comanche history in Spanish Texas, San Antonio de Bexar remained a hotbed for activity. On June 22, 1818, the Penateka Comanche launched a series of forays against the city. The Spanish were able to drive them off, but only after they had lost dozens of horses and several children were captured. These violent incursions became common to Spanish settlers on the frontier and greatly affected the Spaniards' morale.

The last eight years of Spanish rule in colonial Mexico were rife with turmoil that kept royal officials from sending the Penateka Comanche their gifts. These problems also kept Spain from sending troops to the region to control the frontier. As a result, Spanish hide hunters and refugee tribes from central

Texas and the United States entered Comanche territory. Among the refugee tribes were the Creeks, Cherokee, and Choctaw, who all contributed to the decimation of the buffalo herds and, therefore, threatened mass starvation of the Comanche Indians. Coupled with a smallpox epidemic in 1816 that killed an estimated four thousand Comanche, the decrease in buffalo had a detrimental effect on their people. As a result, leading Comanche chiefs, such as Gonique and Barbaquista, favored raids against the Spaniards.

CHAPTER THREE

THE RISE OF VIOLENCE

After a series of revolts that grew out of the increasing political turmoil both in Spain and Mexico, a treaty was signed granting Mexico independence on August 24, 1821. Mexico wanted to strengthen its defenses against illegal American filibustering expeditions and Indian raids. As a result, Stephen F. Austin and his father were granted permission to settle three hundred American families in Texas as a buffer from illegal American incursions and settlement into the area. However, an unforeseen result of this colony was the American's refusal to recognize

Indian claims to land, resulting in increasing tensions and violence with the Indians of the region. Indian concepts of communally owned hunting territories contradicted American ideas of individual land ownership, and the appeal of free and open land and the potential opportunity to accumulate wealth was too strong for the newcomers. Although initial contact with Austin's colonists was peaceful, relationships soon deteriorated, and the Comanche began to distinguish their American trading allies from the Anglos that had settled in Texas. Conflicts arose, raids increased, and unable to get any help from Mexico, Austin enlisted Comanche enemies, such as the Cherokee, Tonkawas, and Lipan Apaches, to attack the Comanche and sell him their stolen horses.

As violence grew, Mexicans and some Comanche groups looked towards amity, and on January 10, 1823, many Penatekas, including Barbaquista, Gonique, and Spirit Talker, visited Mexico City. A treaty was agreed upon and signed, and Mexico and the Penatekas enjoyed peace for a few years. The Comanches pledged to restrain their young men from future forays into Mexico, and in return, Mexico promised to establish trading posts along the Texas frontier. The citizens of San Antonio de Bexar experienced another devastating raid by the Comanche in July of 1825.

Two hundred and twenty-six Comanche men, some traveling with their wives and children, rode into the town where they stayed almost a week. For six days, these Comanches attacked and looted stores and homes, carrying off whatever they wanted. This long episode of terror for the people of San Antonio was not soon forgotten and continued to add to their hatred and fear of the Comanche people. Once again, the Mexicans had to fight the Comanche. In 1827, following a defeat at the hands of a joint force of Mexican soldiers and Lipan Apache, the Penateka Comanche signed a second peace treaty with Mexico.

Consequently, Chief Paruakevitsi visited various Penateka Comanche groups to solicit a united front, and he formalized negotiations in San Antonio that October. Overall, at least for the short term, the treaty was successful, and the Comanche even assisted the Mexicans in a war against the Wichita Indians. In an accident outside San Antonio that threatened an end to their peace, Paruakevitsi was killed by Mexican forces, but many of the Penateka tried to maintain peace with Mexico. As a sign of good faith, the Comanche returned many stolen horses to Mexican officials in San Antonio. While the successes of these meetings kept most of the Comanche from raiding Mexicans or causing more problems in their territory, not all young warriors were concerned with the implications of breaking their peoples' promises, and some smaller raids continued.

Angered at the lack of promised trade and the possibility of personal recognition, young warrior chiefs continued to conduct raids into the Mexican states of Chihuahua, Coahuila, and Nuevo Leon, attacking coaches, kidnapping women, and stealing their horses and mules. As hostility increased, Mexican officials such as Manuel de Mier y Teran ordered Elosua, the ayudante inspector of Coahuila and Texas at San Antonio, to proceed against the Comanche who did not immediately present themselves as friends of Mexico in the San Antonio region. Elosua dispatched Captain Manuel Lafuente with one hundred thirty-two soldiers and sixty-six militiamen to seek hostile Indian groups, such as the Tawakona, Waco, and Comanche. On November 13, 1831, they attacked a Tawakoni village on Cowhouse Creek, where Comanche Chief Barbaquista and his son were killed.

Mexican efforts to rid their land of Comanche ultimately proved unsuccessful. However, although several Comanche groups were still at war with Mexico, many groups continued to solicit peace with the Mexicans until early 1832. Incoroy and other Comanche leaders brought goods like furs, bear grease, and pemmican to San Antonio for trade that year, while unbeknownst to them, Mexican officials were preparing for more campaigns against the Comanche. Hostilities had increased between the Comanche and Mexicans, as well as with other Indian groups in Texas. In 1832, the Apache, Kichais,

Tawakonis, and Tonkawas came together to fight Mexican forces. Coupled with the fact that there was growing unrest among the Anglo population within Texas, Mexico faced a multi-front war. At the same time, Mexico was concerned with preventing an Anglo-American uprising.

Angered that violence still raged in Texas, Mexican officials decided to retaliate against the Penateka Comanche for breaking their promises made in the peace treaty signed a few years before. The Mexicans appealed to the Shawnee Indians for assistance, and a campaign against the Comanche began in early 1832. Camped outside of San Antonio, the Shawnee waited patiently for Comanche Chief Isayona to lead his people out of the city after a visit to trade their goods with the locals. Ambushed, Chief Isayona was killed, and the Penatekas were defeated. Following the assault, Shawnee forces entered San Antonio, requesting additional troops from the Mexicans for another attack against the Comanche. The newly combined force gave chase to the fleeing Comanche, and after a few days, a battle between these groups ensued and resulted in the death of thirty Comanche. The Mexican's Indian policy had shifted, and their new objective was to completely drive the Comanche out of Texas altogether.

Over the next year, the Mexicans were unable to stop the constant attacks and counter-attacks of the Comanche. But while some Comanche continued to raid the Mexicans, others still sought peace. In February 1834, four hundred Comanche traveled to San Antonio, hoping to open a new negotiation to lead these two groups to peace. As a sign of good faith, the Comanche returned one hundred fifty stolen horses and mules taken by young tribesmen. Impressed with this overture and facing a rebellion from their American colonists, Martin Perfecto de Cos, the new Eastern Interior Provinces commanding general, decided to pursue peace. In August of 1835, Cos met with a group of three hundred Comanche in Matamoros and agreed to end hostilities between the two groups.

Relations between the Comanches and Mexico remained strained. Comanches continued to make raids and stole Mexican and Tejano horses and mules, which they traded with Americans in Louisianan. Acting as the middlemen, the Comanche would buy guns and ammunition and trade and arm more westerly tribes, potentially creating more trouble for Mexico. Mexican officials believed these illegal American traders who had set up posts on the Red River were continuing to incite Indians to attack Mexican settlements. For example, there was proof that Holland Coffee met with some Comanche in 1835 and asked them to go into the interior and kill Mexicans and steal their horses and mules for a more lucrative Indian-American trade arrangement. Whatever the case, Comanche-Mexican alliances and relations continued declining despite some apparent successes.

By 1835, the entire frontier was in flames, and both the threat of an Anglo-American revolt as well as an Indian uprising seemed definite. Mexican officials worried the Indians would ally themselves with the Texians and made attempts to stop such an alliance. Until the first significant fighting on October 2, 1835, when Texian revolutionists skirmished with Mexican troops at Gonzales, both the Texians and Mexicans worried that the other had enlisted the Indians of Texas for help.

Such a partnership could have proved crucial for victory. Early in 1836, as war raged in Texas, the provisional government appointed Edward Burleson to lead a commission to arrange a peace treaty with the Comanche of Texas. However, his efforts were unsuccessful because of his limited authority and inability to promise a reservation or permanent frontier home.

Despite initial failures, Texian officials continued to try to enlist Comanche assistance. Southern Comanche groups ignored these efforts, while northern bands stuck to their homesteads for now. In 1837, the Texian government continued to solicit the Comanche and Cherokee Chief Bowl, which was sent to visit the various Comanche bands. Because Texian politicians regarded Comanche hunting lands as public domain and refused to make any concessions the

Comanche sought, Chief Bowl's efforts were also unsuccessful. The Comanche played no role in the Anglo-American effort for independence or in Mexico's struggle to control their rebellious province.

In the years following the Texas Revolution, Comanche raided farther and farther south from Laredo into Matamoros and hindered Mexico's attempts to regain control of the territory. However, their raids throughout Texas complicated Texian efforts to maintain control of their new land and further settle its frontier. Mexico sought new alliances to achieve its goals, and many of its plans involved alliances with the different Indian tribes in Texas, including the Cherokee, who were eventually driven from Texas soil in 1839. The threat of a second Indian war fought on two fronts, was troublesome, and rumors of Mexican-Indian alliances continued to plague the Republic of Texas. The Indians used their power to their advantage and continued to play the Texians and Mexicans off of each other as fears of a second war grew.

Western newspapers reported that the Comanche had declared war on the Texians and would "second the operations of General Santa Anna." Stephen F. Austin himself had written to President Andrew Jackson, charging that "Santa Anna is exciting the Comanches and other Indians who know nothing of law or political division of territory and massacres have been committed in Red River within the United States." Mary Maverick, in her memoirs, noted that "during July 1838, many rumors from the west came to the effect that an army of Centralists was marching to capture Bexar, also that the Comanche nation had entered into a treaty of alliance with the Mexicans and would act with them for our extermination."

In fact, Chief Bowl and a group of militant Cherokees met with General Jose Urrea, the commander of Mexican troops in Matamoros. Bowl claimed that all of the other East Texas tribes, except the Shawnees, Delawares, and the Kickapoos, were ready to fight alongside the Mexicans. As a result, Houston issued a proclamation calling for several East Texas communities to form militias to defend against an Indian uprising. On August 20, 1838, citizens near the Red River killed Don Pedro Julian Miracle, and a diary running from May 1829 to August 11, 1838, was found on his body. In these papers were more incriminating evidence of an attempted conspiracy among the Indians against the Texians. Later, on May 18, 1839, Lieutenant James O. Rice and seventeen men of Captain M. Andrew's company of Texas Rangers attacked a party of twenty to thirty Indians and Mexicans on the San Gabriel Fork of Little River, twenty-five miles from Austin. Three men were killed by the Texians, one of which was Manuel Flores, a Mexican. On Flores' body, more papers were found that alluded to a plot to get the Indians to start a general war against the Texians. The plan called for the Mexicans to simultaneously attack the Republic at the start of a general Indian uprising. It was well known that the Cherokees had visited Mexico and talked with them more than once between 1836 and 1838. The Mexicans had lured the Indians with the guarantee of future possession of their hunting grounds in Texas, something the natives highly desired.

The Texians were facing multiple enemies to the west and south, and the possibility of their collaboration would have made it difficult for the settlers to fight a two-front war. As the dominant Native American force in the southern plains, the Comanche posed the most serious threat to settlers. As "Lords of the Plains," their excellent horsemanship allowed them to master the art of hit-and-run tactics. They would usually travel by night and attack isolated homesteads and ranches on the outskirts of towns, sometimes carrying off livestock and captives. As a result, companies of Rangers were formed to patrol the routes the Comanche were known to take. Many of these encounters are remembered in early Texas sagas, like the attack on Fort Parker, where several American settlers were killed and five taken captive, including the famous nine-year-old Cynthia Parker.

Texian leaders such as Houston worked diligently to establish peace between the Republic and the native populations but to no avail. Houston's peace efforts with the Comanche were hampered because the Texas Congress refused to agree to a boundary line, defining their space and the edge of Texas settlement. Hostility continued, and no peace was known until the Council House Fight in 1840.

Chapter Four
THE PRACTICE OF CAPTIVE

The practice of captive-taking among the North American Indians goes back to prehistoric times and continued to incite great fear among the American settlers of Texas. The first instance in Texas also correlates with the first Europeans who appeared in the territory in 1528 when Alvar Nunez Cabeza de Vaca and three other survivors of the expedition of Panfilo de Narvaez were taken hostage. Throughout the years, captives became another important item to be taken away during the numerous raids that were committed against the Spanish, Mexicans, other Indians, and Americans by the native peoples. They became a major issue for the growing Anglo population in the late 1830s, which led directly to the Council House Fight.

The men, women, and children that were captured by the Indians were taken for different reasons. Some were abducted to replenish the losses suffered during warfare. Others were taken to be tortured in the spirit of revenge against anyone the Indians viewed as an enemy. Captives were also taken for ransom or to gain bargaining power with another group. Once held, many captives, if not killed, were rescued or ransomed by Texas Rangers, soldiers, Indian agents, or traders. But the high prices or goods that were paid to ransom some of these captives only served to increase the "incentive for [future] abductions" of Euroamericans by the Indians. Texians were very fearful of being taken hostage by

Indians, and this served as the motivation for many retaliatory raids and attacks on the native peoples of Texas. In a letter to President Mirabeau B. Lamar in June 1840, A. M. M. Upshaw demonstrated how some American captives were treated among the Comanche a few months earlier. He wrote, "One of the principal men of the Chickawas went last winter on a trading expedition to the Comanche, where he saw several white prisoners...he says that the prisoners are women and boys all of which are in a reached [wretched?] condition."

The vicious cycle of retaliatory attacks between the Texian colonists and the Comanche created a very unstable frontier. As years passed and the Republic of Texas was established, many native groups sought peace as often as war. In the years leading up to the Council House Fight, many of these episodes became essential to understanding the atmosphere among the colonists and Indians in Texas. In early 1836, several Western newspapers reported that the "Comanches have declared war against Texas." In February 1838, one hundred Penateka Comanche entered San Antonio to invite the Texians to travel to the Hill Country to discuss peace between the two groups. Moseley Baker, a member of the Texas Congress, accompanied the group to their encampment on the Colorado River.

There, he met with fifteen headmen and noted that the Comanche had made a declaration for a boundary line, defining their territorial limits. They claimed nearly a quarter of the "finest country in Texas...the territory north and west of the Guadalupe Mountains, extending from the Red River to the Rio Grande." Though they sought peace, they "would listen to no terms unless the government secured the full and undisturbed possession" of the land north of the divide between the Colorado and the Guadalupe rivers west of Bastrop. More terms were discussed, and they agreed to return to San Antonio to finalize the treaty later. Such a promise, if ever actually considered, which it likely was not, would require government authorization. Houston received notice of these negotiations from Robert A. Irion in March, detailing Colonel Henry Karnes's event report, and sought further guidance from Houston for the planned future engagement.

Karnes was described as a short, red-headed man, uneducated, modest, and generous. His name, she said, should incite terror among Indians. Karnes had been held captive by the Comanche years before. Karnes reported to Irion that he was fearful that the

Texian motives had been misrepresented by the Mexicans and Americans to the Comanche, who were told "that our only objective is to acquire land unjustly." Karnes further stated that he did not want to reinforce these perceptions by making false promises to them. They wanted a boundary line, and Karnes reported that they said they would kill all the surveyors on their land who were already operating within their claimed territory.

In his letter to Houston, Irion noted, "The Commissioner of the Land Office has issued orders instructing surveyors to confine their operations...which, if obeyed, may prevent intrusion upon the Indian territory." Colonel Karnes also reported a conspiracy among the Indians of Texas. He feared the Shawnees were working among them, trying to draw the Comanche into an alliance and "influence their minds against the Texians." Last of all, Irion's letter informed Houston that Karnes planned to meet the Comanche when they reported back to San Antonio, present them with gifts, negotiate "without indicating the precise limits of the territory which will be secured to them," and assure the Indians that the Texians had no intention of hurting them or taking away their rights.

Chiefs Eswacany and Essomanny led an embassy of one-hundred fifty to San Antonio in May of 1838 to meet with Texas officials. The Comanche's only demand was a boundary line, but the Texians refused to discuss it. Realizing nothing would happen to these negotiations, the Comanche accepted a few customary gifts and left the city. At the same time, negotiations were going on with the Comanche in San Antonio, and negotiations were also going on with another group of

Penateka Comanche in Bastrop County. Led by Chief Muguara and a few warriors, they appeared at Coleman's Fort on Walnut Creek, asking for a commissioner to be sent to their camp to discuss a treaty. Noah Smithwick, a Ranger officer, was sent with the embassy back to Muguara's village on the Colorado River. Once there, Muguara complained to Smithwick that the Texians were invading their territory, "building houses and fences, and the buffalo get frightened and leave and never come back, and the Indians are left to starve...if the white men would draw a line defining their claims and keep on their side of it the red men would not molest them." Smithwick regrettably informed Muguara that he had no authority to authorize such a treaty, which was often the problem. He asked the Comanche to meet with Texas President Houston in Houston, the Republic of Texas' capital.

In May of 1838, a Comanche delegation of approximately one hundred met in Houston to finalize the terms of a treaty between the two groups. Texian who saw the Comanche entrance into the city described their observations to local papers. Spanish legends of the Comanche attributed a reputation of bravery and ferocity to these Indians of Texas, but that was not what these citizens saw.

The June 1838 Houston Telegraph and May 30, 1838, Texas Register printed the comments of these Texians, who reported that the Comanche looked like "diminutive, squalid, half-naked, poverty-stricken savages... mounted on wretched horses and mules." These descriptions could depict a people in a declining state, or could be reflective of the Texians' racially prejudiced views of the Indians they perceived as inferior or possibly could be a combination of the two.

By May 29, the "Treaty of Peace and Amity" was secured. Present at the negotiations were Irion as Secretary of State, Ashbel Smith as Commissioner on the part of the Republic of Texas, and Comanche chiefs Muguara, Muestyah, and Muhy. Despite Muguara's insistence, the treaty did not identify or mention Comanche land holdings. In the treaty, the Comanche "promised to bring to just punishment such individuals of their tribe as may commit any depredations upon the property or injure the persons of any of the Citizens belonging to the Republic of Texas." They pledged to trade only with appointed trade agents and to keep them safe. They also agreed to meet with the President of Texas on the second Monday of every October. In the treaty, the Comanche were also obligated to restore any stolen goods, and they promised to stop stealing, raiding, and killing livestock. They also agreed to ally with the

Texians and help fight their enemies, including other Indians. They were asked to wear a star to identify themselves to their Texian friends and show that they would not kill or steal from the whites.

Furthermore, the Texians made some minor concessions as well. They pledged to appoint an agent for the Comanche to "superintend their business and protect their rights." The Texians also promised to punish "any citizen of the Republic according to Law, who may in any way infringe on the rights of the said Comanche or injure them in any way whatsoever," as long as the Comanche kept their end of the bargain. Last but not least, the Texians promised to restore stolen goods and prevent further raids upon the Comanche. When it was over, and before the natives departed the city, Houston gave the Comanche gifts, including a white flag representing peace and a passport that read these Indians were "friends and brothers of the Texians."

The treaty proved completely ineffectual. The Comanche were angered that the Texians would not delineate a boundary line. As a result, the Comanche killed a few traders who traveled to their village, and a series of skirmishes ensued. According to citizens of San Felipe, this same band stole several horses near San Antonio not long after these peace talks concluded. Mary Maverick recorded an incident on June 29, 1838, in which thirty-eight Comanches came to the edge of town (San Antonio), killed two Mexicans, and stole one boy. She also noted that on June 13, a German and another Mexican had been killed by the local Comanche. In August, Texas Rangers fought a group of Penateka Comanche near the Medina

River. On August 10, Colonel Karnes attacked a party of two hundred Comanche at Arroyo Seco and reportedly killed Essomanny. On September 8, approximately seventy Comanche, angry about the events at Arroyo Seco and seeking peace with the Texians, visited Bastrop. On October 20, 1838, Texian surveyors were attacked by the Comanche west of San Antonio. Thirteen Texians responded and were quickly surrounded; eight Texians were killed, and four were wounded. Five days later, the Battle at the Anadarko Village ensued, and Chief Esawacany was reportedly killed. Penateka Comanches, reportedly of Muguara's band, also raided settlements along the Guadalupe River, where thirteen-year-old Matilda Lockhart was abducted. Numerous skirmishes plagued the frontier, and other Comanche parties raided various settlements in Texas and Mexico, kidnapping women and children and stealing horses and other livestock. Finally, on December 21, 1838, a bill was passed to establish a regiment of over eight hundred men for the "further protection of the frontier against the Comanches and the other Indians."

The act also provided for eight companies of mounted Ranger volunteers. By the end of 1838, the Treaty of May 29 had been completely forgotten by the Penateka Comanche and the Texians. However, the Indians were not the only culprits for the decline of the Comanche and Texian treaties and relationships. The Texians also played a role, and Texian forces, in conjunction with Indian auxiliaries, waged brutal warfare against the Penateka on the Western frontier. Attitudes worsened when Mirabeau B. Lamar was elected president and initiated a campaign of extinction. On Feb. 15, 1839,

John H. Moore, sixty-two other whites, and Chief Cuelgas de Castro's fifteen Lipans attacked Muguara's camp. In Moore's report to Secretary of War Albert Sidney Johnston, he said he led three volunteer companies formed under the government authorization of the 25th of January to "proceed against the Comanche and other hostile Indians in our northwest frontier." He further reported that on the 13th, his spies, a Lipan hunting party, discovered an Indian encampment on a small stream called Spring Creek, a tributary of the San Saba River. The companies marched under the cover of timber and waited until after sunset to move closer. After daybreak, against Castro's advice, Moore dismounted most of his men and attacked the village. He ordered the Lipans on horseback to stampede the caballado on the left flank. The La Grange Company, under the command of William M. Eastland, formed the right wing, and the

Bastrop Company, under Noah Smithwick's command, attacked the center of the village, "slaughtering the enemy in their beds." The Indians soon recovered and retreated to a deep rut. After several failed attempts to counter-attack the Texians, finally, a white flag was brought to Moore's men by a man and a woman, and a conversation ensued.

The Indians said they had five prisoners and wished to exchange them for the Indians captured during the fight. They claimed to have had one middle-aged woman, a fifteen-year-old thought to be Matilda Lockhart (daughter of Andrew Lockhart, a member of one of Moore's companies), and the other three were presumed to be the three children kidnapped in the same place as Matilda. But unknown to the Texians was the fact that the Comanche captured by the Lipans had already been executed, and no exchange could be made. The Lipans also walked away with ninety-three horses and forty-six mules. After the news, the Comanche warned the Texians that their numbers were increasing, and they were working with the Shawnee against the Republic. In reporting the event, Moore said that his enemy's loss "must have been considerable...very great" and that the Texians only lost one man in Battle and another from a mortal wound a short time later.

The Penateka responded by attacking settlements along the frontier, but by summer, the Texas forces forced Penateka bands to retreat to the Colorado River. In the fall, smallpox reduced the already declining number of people by killing a large number of Indians. Weakened, some bands decided to pursue peace with the Texians. Historian John Henry Brown suggests that there may have been another treaty between the Texians and Comanche after this event. He insinuates that the number of hostages recovered from Indian captivity in the winter of 1839-1840 demonstrates the presence of a treaty. Still, the details of any such treaty, or the ransoming of captives, are unknown today.

In Maverick's memoirs, she alone recorded another incident between the Comanche Indians and the Texians that further helps to understand the mindsets of both parties at the time of the Council House Fight in the spring of 1840. She recalled an event just before March when ten visiting Americans and ten Mexicans visited the countryside before returning home. Just after sunset, Mr. "Talking" Campbell, a party member, returned to town, reporting that the Comanche had gotten between the party and San Antonio, blocking their path back. He said that he had a fast horse and could get through unharmed.

The next morning, another party from San Antonio went out to find their friends and found their dead bodies, naked and hacked with tomahawks. In addition to their mutilation at the hands of the Indians, they had also been partly eaten by wolves throughout the night.

Conflict between the Texians and the Comanche had been growing since the European settlement of the territory. Neither the Comanche nor Texians understood each other's values or organization, leading to increased conflict between the two parties even while many sought peace. The days, weeks, and years leading up to the Council House Fight were rife with hostility. Not only had the Comanche brutally waged war on the Texians and continued to appear to break their promises with the settlers, but the Texians had also waged a counter-war on the natives and did very little to develop any lasting peaceful solutions.

Chapter Five
THE COUNCIL HOUSE FIGHT

Years of contact with the Indians of Texas lead to many violent encounters and ultimately to their expulsion from the state of Texas. The Comanche had been the greatest threat to settlers of the plains, and continued attempts to create peace failed, resulting in renewed hostilities. While many Comanche bands and individuals continued to raid Texian settlements, others, weakened by disease and warfare, sought peace. One of the latter was the Penataka, and their apparent effort to secure a negotiated peace led to one of the bloodiest clashes between Indians and

Texians in the history of the Republic of Texas.

On January 9, 1840, three Comanche and their Mexican captives rode into San Antonio, seeking peace between the Texians and their group of Penateka Comanche. At this time, a small white boy, presumed to be John Horn, was also given to the Texians. The Comanche came to the town center and called for Col. Henry Karnes, whom they knew from his previous captivity, fights, and past peace negotiations. San Antonio was the largest community within a reasonable distance of their villages and was a likely place for the Comanche to meet with the Texians. It was a site of previous peace negotiations and possessed the manufactured goods the Indians desired. The possible motivations for seeking a lasting peace have been attributed to many factors, such as the losses caused by smallpox, retaliation raids made by the Texians, as well as apparent threats made to the Comanche by warriors from the Arapaho and Cheyenne Indians.

It most likely combined all these factors and their effects on their people. Their power in the region was declining, and though they might not have really wanted to make serious concessions to the Texians, they realized it was the only way to survive. Varying levels of opposition to submitting to the Texians among the Comanche are evident in the continual light and isolated resistance on the frontier following these talks. Among the Comanche delegation in San Antonio that day, the most distinguished one appeared to be a "priest." The apparent religious leader told the Texians that eighteen days prior, a General Council of the Penateka Comanche had convened and agreed to seek a truce with the Republic of

Texas. The man, who claimed to have been deputed by the council to solicit peace, told Karnes "that the nation will accept of Peace on any terms, being sensible of their inability to contend with the Texas forces." Furthermore, he affirmed his people's desire to work with the Texians. He demonstrated their dedication to the peace process by detailing their defiance of efforts among the Cherokee and Mexicans to "stir up a general war" against the Texians.

Karnes demanded that for any negotiations to take place, the Comanche must release all their American captives, which the Texians estimated at thirteen. The Texians also demanded that the Comanche abandon Central Texas, cease interfering with Texas incursions, and avoid all white settlements. A future negotiation date was agreed upon, and initial peace terms were finalized. In twenty to thirty days, a large delegation, including the principal chiefs, would return to the city with all their white captives and negotiate a lasting truce. Karnes reported that he treated the Indians well and gave them their customary gifts before exiting the city. In Colonel Karnes' report of the event to the Secretary of War, Albert Sidney Johnston, he noted that the Penatekas' "known treachery and duplicity induces me to put little faith in them."

Oddly enough, Karnes claimed that the delegation of Penateka Comanche was too large to take hostage. Taking a group captive and proposing future peace negotiations was not common, and his apparent apology is concerning and confusing. Maverick offered one explanation, "this was the third time these Indians had come for a talk pretending to seek peace and trying to get ransom money for their American and Mexican captives." Knowing of this past deception might serve to better understand Karnes' motivations here. But if these men were considered dangerous enough to take into custody, why would Karnes have given them gifts upon their departure? Was his first goal to incarcerate the Indians, and because it would not feasibly work, was a peace treaty a suitable alternative to him?

Furthermore, Karnes requested that one or two commissioners be sent to San Antonio to better secure and negotiate peace with the Comanche. He asked that they be accompanied by a "force sufficient to justify our seizing and retaining [them] as hostages," if needed. The Texians had the upper hand in the discussions, risking the loss of nothing of real substance to the Indians. Still, because of past failures and blunders, certain reasonable precautions both parties took were understandable.

Upon receiving the report from Colonel Karnes, Secretary of War Johnston chose two commissioners, Adjunct General Hugh McLeod and Col. William G. Cooke, to negotiate peace with the Penateka Comanche band that had requested the truce. Johnston ordered the men to inform the Indians that the Republic "assumes the right, about all Indian Tribes residing within the limits of the Republic, to dictate the conditions of such residence" and that they should live accordingly, and only then would they be granted the peace that they so desperately sought. He also ordered the commissioners to inform the Comanche that the citizens of the Republic had the right to occupy any vacant lands without the fear of an Indian raid into any of their communities.

Johnston clearly stated that it was essential that the Comanche understood that they were "prohibited from entering our settlements." His continued distrust of the Comanche also led the Secretary of War to order Lt. Col. William S. Fisher to lead three infantry companies to San Antonio to await the arrival of the Penateka Comanche. These companies were drawn from Edward Burleson's Frontier Regiment, which had been disbanded before the holidays. He further ordered Fisher to seize the Indians if all of their American captives were not returned to the Texians as promised.

If that happened, the Texians were to allow the leaders to send messengers back to their village and secure the release of the remaining captives. If all American prisoners were eventually freed, so too would the Texians free Comanche captives. This plan had never been attempted before by the Spanish, Mexicans, or the Texians. But, this would all be avoided if the Penatekas brought all of their captives: "They will therefore be received with kindness and permitted to depart without molestation," and the troops would not be used. Johnston also noted that he was aware that gift-giving was usually a custom when negotiations were pursued with the Indians but that the practice should be done away with in the future. This is a curious statement for a man pursuing peace with the Comanche.

It appears that Johnston understood the Texians' advantage over the Indians, and, in a slightly risky political and diplomatic maneuver, he refused to cooperate with them any more than was absolutely necessary. The orders were issued, and the commissioners and the troops left for San Antonio.

In San Antonio, on March 19, 1840, the Día de San Jose, two Comanche scouts, arrived to inform the commissioners of the approaching Indians. Soon after, sixty-five Comanche men, women, and children entered San Antonio with only one American prisoner. Leading the delegation was a bald-headed medicine man, Muguara, who had worked with the Texians before with the failed Treaty in May of 1829. Not only did Karnes, who had lived among the Penateka as a captive, confirm this, but Noah Smithwick, a familiar character in early Texian/ Indian episodes, had also lived among Muguara's band and recognized him as well. In fact, Smithwick had spent over three months living with the Comanche, trying to secure another treaty that had never been signed. Muguara was elected the main peace chief by the Penateka General Council, which had been formed not long before they came to San Antonio.

Isomania was the worst of the depredating chiefs and was not present that day. This information creates little controversy and could be easily explained in several ways. While it may add to the knowledge of which chiefs were not there, it does not contradict what has always been reported, that these men were the principal civil chiefs. There is no way of knowing just how many different bands of Penatekas gathered in general council days before, and these chiefs could have represented a group not as well known to the Texians but still highly respected among the Comanche. It could be explained simply by further examining the social structure of the Comanche, as previously discussed.

The general council could have chosen the peace chiefs among them to represent their peaceful interests to the Texians. The peace delegation of the Penateka Comanche brought with them only one white captive, fifteen-year-old Matilda Lockhart, and one young Mexican boy. As the delegation entered the camp, Matilda, the young captive of the Penateka, was being used as a herder for their extra ponies. She had been captured in December of 1838 with her younger sister and possibly with two other children of her family. Two unsuccessful excursions were made to free the young captives, one to the head of the Guadalupe River in late 1838 and another by John Moore in 1839 to Spring Creek.

When Matilda was handed over to the Texians, she was in a "frightful condition." She told them stories of sexual and physical abuse and accused her captives of great torture. Matilda appeared very bad and described that "her head, arms, and face were full of bruises and sores, and her nose actually was burnt off to the bone, all the fleshy end gone and a great scab formed on the end of the base. Both nostrils were wide-open and denuded of flesh." Furthermore, she told Maverick that the Indians beat her and would "wake her from sleep by sticking a chunk of fire to her flesh, especially to her nose, and now they would shout and laugh like fiends when she cried."

Matilda was embarrassed about her condition and did not want to be seen. Her scars were severe and probably sickening, and most likely, people were staring at them. The Comanche typically treated captives very brutally to instill a sense of fear in their prisoners. Matilda was taken to Maverick's home, where she was bathed, dressed, and cared for until her brother picked her up a few days later.

When questioned, Matilda claimed there were other white captives that the Comanches had not brought and that the Indians planned to ransom them in the following days. In his letter to President Lamar reporting the day's events, McLeod noted that Matilda seemed to be a very intelligent girl. He repeated that Matilda claimed she had seen several other white captives that the Penateka Comanche were holding several days before at their principal camp.

Presumably, this is the same camp assembled to authorize the delegation that first came into San Antonio several days earlier seeking peace between the two groups. She further explained that the Indians were going to demand a "high price for her" and bring in the rest of their American captives one at a time. In Maverick's memoirs, she goes into more depth than McLeod does in his report to President Lamar describing the situation. Maverick claimed that the

Comanche wanted the Texians to send traders to their camp with "paint, powder, flannel, blankets, and such other articles as they should name to ransom the other captives." According to her, there was precedent for this type of arrangement. Previously, the Comanche had asked for particular goods in exchange for their American captives, and they were brought directly to their camp by Texian officials. When tragedy struck, and smallpox killed several Indians, the Texian traders were blamed for the epidemic and killed. Incidents like this only weakened Texian trust in the Comanche and made them more suspicious of their promises. Maverick also noted that Matilda never really recovered from her ordeal and survived no more than two or three more years.

After Matilda was presented to the Texians as the Comanche's one and only

American captive, the twelve principal chiefs were directed toward the local jail. Attached to the jail was a council room that was part of the courthouse originally built in the 1740s. The complex was known as the Casas Reales. It had once been the official residence for Juan Maria Vicencio de Ripperda, the first Spanish governor of Texas to make his headquarters in San Antonio (which in 1770 was known as San Fernando de Bexar). It had also once been the home of the prisoners of the Philip Nolan expedition. The one-story stone courthouse was on the corner of Main Plaza and Calabosa (Market) Street. As negotiations began, outside the council house in the courtyard (which later became the City Market in Market Street), the other warriors amused themselves and the townspeople who had gathered by shooting their bows and arrows at different targets.

Other curious citizens, including Maverick and her friend Lucinda Higginbotham, watched from the safety of their homes. Once assembled in the council house, the principal Chief, Muguara, was asked about the other captives. It was Muguara himself who had days before promised to return all of the Penateka's American captives. The Chief responded by telling the Texians that Matilda was their only hostage, and the others belonged to other bands, therefore out of his authority or jurisdiction. If it is presumed that the principal camp assembled several days before the Penatekas had first entered San Antonio, it was the same camp that Matilda remembers.

All the tribes present were represented by Muguara, his authority, and his promises made to the Texians. So when he entered San Antonio on March 19, 1840, without all their

American captives, he had broken his promise that was essential to their peace talks and the possibility of entering into a treaty with the Texians. To add to his apparent dishonesty, Muguara further acknowledged that they had violated all their previous treaties with the Texians and, tauntingly, demanded that new confidence be reposed in this situation. After the Chief's assurance that there were no other captives under his custody, he responded, "How do you like that answer?" It is unknown if Muguara made such a statement if it was misinterpreted or even misunderstood. However, it was perceived as a negative, even sarcastic remark that heightened the tension in the room.

Lieutenant Colonel Fisher was then ordered to march his companies into the immediate vicinity of the Council House. The Texians again confronted the twelve

Comanche chiefs inside the council room. They decided the chiefs had to be detained by Secretary of War Johnson's orders and Colonel Karnes' recommendations. McLeod noted that it was "the only alternative left us." The Texians had a Tejano interpreter who knew Comanche, and he was asked to relay the message of their detainment to the chiefs. Aware of the outrage that would result on behalf of the Penatekas, the interpreter slowly moved toward the door and exited immediately after delivering the Texians' message.

The chiefs were informed they could return several young men to their camp to retrieve the other captives. The Texians further explained to the Indians that they would not be released until the captives were safely returned to San Antonio. Capt. George T. Howard's company was ordered into the council room and the adjoining room in the back near the courtyard, where the other Comanche warriors were. Once inside, he placed sentinels at the doors and across the room to act as their guards. There were no more negotiations to be made between the two groups at that time, and Texian officials descended from the platform.

Chapter Six

THE CLASH

The chiefs tried to follow the exiting Texian officials out of the building. It was in those next few moments that the Penatekas decided to fight rather than submit to the Texians and their detainment. One sprang to the back door and attempted to pass the sentinel, who presented his musket to the Chief to stop his escape. When stopped, the Comanche chief apparently stabbed the sentinel in his side, though some have suggested the enraged Chief stabbed the sentinel before being presented with his weapon. Captain Howard tried to stop another escaping Penateka and also received a stab to his side. As he fell to the ground, Howard ordered a soldier to shoot his attacker, who was killed immediately. By this time, all of the Indian chiefs had drawn their bows and presented their knives to the Texians still in the room, ready to continue the fight that had already begun. Colonel Fisher ordered his men in the council house to "fire if they do not desist," then the Indians rushed the Texian troops in a last attempt to escape their captivity. Now under attack, the troops were ordered to "fire!" Within a very short time, fighting subsided inside the room, and all twelve of the Penateka Comanche chiefs lay dead.

Before the council room could be cleared, Captain Howard and his men were ordered to the front of the building complex to cut off any attempted retreat in that direction. The wound he received moments earlier was severe, and Captain Gillen was ordered to relieve Howard of his command for the remainder of the affair. As the fight ended inside the Council House, it was just beginning outside. Captain William D. Redd's Company A was stationed in the courtyard to watch the other Comanche warriors. Upon hearing the war whoops inside the Council House, the Indians became immediately aware of their leader's trouble.

Mary Maverick noted that the whoops were "so loud, so shrill, and so inexpressibly horrible" and that it was hard for the Texians to comprehend its implications quickly. The warriors understood instantly and immediately attacked the Texians in the yard, killing Judge Thomson. As pandemonium erupted, many Penatekas fled and were shot in their backs and killed while escaping across the river. The few Indians that actually made it across encountered a small party of mounted men under the command of Colonel Lysander Wells. Riding north on Soledad Street, Colonel Wells was elegantly dressed and mounted on an equally impressive horse. He was not yet aware of the degeneration of negotiations and was just as surprised as the Indians when they met one another. Wells was attacked by a fleeing Comanche who tried to take over his horse's reins.

Colonel Wells shot and killed his attacker almost immediately, but the April 22, 1840, Telegraph and Texas Register reported differently. The paper claimed that Wells had a new Colt Revolver that would not fire because the wedge was improperly placed. Furthermore, it said that his Indian attacker grabbed his gun and, in the ensuing struggle, was able to take it away from Wells. Luckily for the Colonel, one of his men came to his aid and was able to kill the Indian. The papers reported that Wells "sat back in his saddle and cursed the Comanche and Sam Colt in equal measure." Eventually, all the fleeing Indians were killed or captured, except one renegade Mexican who was allowed to escape.

Citizens and soldiers of the Republic fought with the Comanche, and desperate fights between the Penatekas and the Texians sprang up all over town. Several Indians sought refuge, barricaded themselves in nearby stone houses, and continued to fight. One warrior, possibly two, fled inside Higginbotham's kitchen and refused any request to surrender made to him by the Texians through some of the captured Comanche women. In McLeod's letter to Lamar, he claimed that the barricaded Indian killed and wounded several of the Texians, which is possible but highly unlikely. His people might have been partly responsible, but not all the men dead were killed by the Indians--some Anglos died due to friendly fire. It is more likely that McLeod justified the Texians' next course of action concerning this particular warrior. Shortly after midnight, the Texians climbed on top of the home, and Anton Lockmar and another man dropped a blazing candlewick ball soaked in turpentine through a hole made in the roof. Scared, or perhaps injured by the object dropped, the Indian exited Higginbotham's home and was immediately shot and killed.

The Texian troops were stationed in San Antonio for the fateful day, and the other citizen soldiers immediately sprang to action when they were not required to, demonstrating the Texian tradition and societal demands placed upon the settlers living on the frontier. Many Texians at the

Battle are known from other early Texas and Ranger history events. Captain Matthew "Old Paint" Caldwell was visiting San Antonio from Gonzales and took part in the fighting in a private capacity. He was unarmed and was shot through the right leg. Mary Maverick notes in her memoirs that it was presumed he was injured by the first volley of shots fired by the Texian soldiers and not Indians. It was also reported that Caldwell took a gun away from an Indian, killed him, and beat another Indian with the end of his gun after it had broken. Another tale has Captain Caldwell throwing rocks at the Indians when he finds himself unarmed and in a raging battle. Other accounts, more likely than some of the previous stories, have John Dabney Morris as Caldwell's savior, shooting an Indian before he was able to shoot his already aimed weapon at the unarmed Caldwell.

Whatever the truth, his presence at this event was significant for his future career, credibility, and legend. A soon-to-be Ranger, Michael H. Chevallie, was also present. Chevallie was an army lieutenant who managed to get Mary Maverick to safety when she was caught unprotected outside her gates during the street battle. John Hemphill also fought against the Comanche that day in San Antonio. Years later, he would gain fame as one of the seven elected delegates from Texas to the Provisional Confederate Congress. Another young visitor, C. Y. Cayce, had been outside the front door when negotiations degenerated. He was killed almost immediately after the fighting began.

Lieutenant William M. Dunnington was also killed during the conflict by a Comanche woman who shot an arrow through his body. It was reported that after he was shot,

Dunnington fired and killed his attacker. The Texas Sentinel, on April 15, 1840, stated, "Her brains bespattered the wall; he turned around and exclaimed, 'I have killed him, but I believe he has killed me, too,' and fell and expired in twenty minutes." He was unaware that the warrior was a female because she was dressed like a man.

In the end, a total of thirty-five Indians, as well as seven Texians, were killed. Of the Comanche, three were women, two were children, twelve were principal chiefs, and the remainder were young male warriors. Included in the dead were Muguara, SpiritTalker, Eagle, and the father of Sanaco, later Chief of a group of Penateka Comanche who visited the Clear Fork Reservation in 1856. All of the remaining twenty-seven Indians were captured and imprisoned save one, who was sent back to the Comanche camp to secure the release of the remaining white captives. The Texians lost an officer, two soldiers, and four civilians, while only three officers, one private, and four civilians were wounded.

Chapter Seven
A BIG MISTAKE

The Council House Fight was also a major military and diplomatic blunder for both parties. Both had ample reasons to distrust each other and take extra precautions, including fighting back and defending themselves. Neither group planned or foresaw what occurred on March 19, 1840, yet they were both to blame. The Comanche remained one of the most, if not the most, threatening groups to Euro-American expansion in Texas, and their apparent deception had angered the Texians. Likewise, when negotiations soured, and the chiefs were informed of their detainment, it served as sufficient cause for the Indians to strike back. Both groups considered the other to be at fault, and each felt forced by the other's actions. The Texians entered a twelve-day truce with the captured Comanches. At their request, a Comanche captive, the widow of a fallen chief, was released to journey back to their main camp to report the events of the day and secure the release of the other American captives still in their possession. Only after she returned with these hostages would the Indians captured by the Texians be freed. It was Spirit Talker's widow that was sent back to her people to recover the remaining white captives. She claimed she could return in four days with the captives, but twelve days was granted to provide her sufficient time.

The Texians warned the woman that if she did not return in the given time, they would assume the American hostages had already been killed by the Comanche in retaliation for their chiefs' deaths. The Texians would be forced to kill the Penateka captives.

The woman was well mounted, given provisions, and sent off. Both McLeod and Colonel Cooke remained in San Antonio to await her return, and when she did not return in the prearranged twelve days, the Texians assumed the worst. All of the Texian's Comanche captives were eventually moved from the city jail to the San Jose Mission and then to Camp Cooke at the head of the San Antonio River. Many of the people of San Antonio went to see them, and many felt very bad about their situation. They were treated kindly and were hired into local homes to live and work. And while some Indians were ransomed and exchanged, the rest managed to escape one way or another. Just after the

Council House Fight, on March 26, 1840, Webster came into San Antonio with her three-year-old daughter on her back. Mary Maverick noted that she looked like an Indian dressed in buckskin; her hair was cut square across her forehead, and her exposed skin was sunburned dark. As she appeared in the city, Webster yelled that she had just escaped the captivity of the citizens in the street. She had been wandering for several days and had no knowledge of the Council House Fight or what had occurred there several days before. Webster was taken to John W. Smith's house, where she and her daughter were fed. Then, five ladies, including Mrs. Jacques, Mrs. Elliot, Mrs. Smith, Mrs. Higginbotham, and Mrs. Maverick, bathed Mrs. Webster and took care of her for the next several weeks. During this time, she told these ladies about where she had come from and what had happened to her before captivity.

Webster, her husband, their four children, and two African Americans came to Texas from Virginia in 1838 and traveled to their newly built home northwest of Austin in August. Just north of their home, they camped one night at Brushy Creek, where a party of Penateka Comanche attacked them. All of the men were killed in the ensuing Battle, and Webster, as well as her ten- and two-year-old children, were captured. Her "infant was taken from her arms, and its brains dashed out on a tree, and her second child was killed." Both Webster and her son, Booker, were tied to horses.

Webster had "held her child of two years so tightly and pled for it so piteously that the Indians left it with her." The three were taken into the mountains, where Booker was stripped and shaved and adopted into the family of an old woman who had recently lost her child. Soon after their arrival, Booker came down with "brain fever" or meningitis, and his new mother nursed him back to health. The Indians had allowed Webster to keep her daughter but had prohibited any contact with her son, Booker. The Indians worked Webster, made her cook, and stake out the tribe's ponies. Maverick claims she was beaten, but new scholars have questioned the authenticity of this accusation, citing the lack of evidence.

After approximately nineteen months of captivity, Webster was finally able to escape. She learned of the Comanche's proximity to San Antonio, and after a long day's work, she slipped away under the cover of night with her daughter on her back.

The Comanche were deeply angered by the events in San Antonio, viewing the attack on their ambassadors as a violation of diplomatic immunity, which significantly soured their perception of the Texians. Following the Council House Fight, both groups made efforts to free captives held by the other, leading to the release of several individuals but ultimately contributing to the decline of Comanche dominance in the Texas Plains. On March 28, a large Penateka Comanche, led by Isamini, rode to San Antonio, where Isamini provocatively entered the town, taunting and challenging the residents. Despite their bravado, the Comanche left for the San José Mission after being informed of the presence of Texian soldiers. At the mission, Captain William D. Redd, who had taken over command after Lt. Col. William S. Fisher was injured, informed Isamini of a truce. Despite Redd's willingness to fight after the truce ended, Isamini insulted him but ultimately refrained from engaging, while the Texian soldiers were restrained to prevent them from initiating a fight.

A non-commissioned officer, Lysander Wells, criticized Captain William D. Redd in a letter, accusing him of cowardice for not engaging the Comanche. The letter, signed by several others, infuriated Redd, who then challenged Wells to a duel. Shortly after Lt. Col. Fisher decided to move his forces from the San José Mission to the Alamo, Redd, and Wells met for their duel at dawn. Both men were fatally wounded; Redd died instantly from a shot to the head, and Wells succumbed to his injuries two weeks later. This loss was particularly tragic for the Frontier Regiment, as both men had fought at the Battle of San Jacinto. They were buried near Milam Square in San Antonio. In the weeks following these events, conflicting accounts emerged about negotiations between the Comanche and the

Texians. While Mary Maverick's memoirs and Captain George T. Howard's report differ in details, Howard's account is considered more reliable closer to the negotiations. On April 3, 1840, two Comanche, including a chief named Pivia, entered San Antonio to propose a prisoner exchange per the agreed twelve-day truce. Temporarily in command, Howard instructed Pivia to bring the Texian prisoners into town, initiating the exchange. On April 5, Howard brought additional troops to San Antonio to secure the release of the remaining American captives.

Further negotiations between the Texians and the Comanche led to the decision to send two San Antonio citizens, Damasio and Antonio Perez, to the Comanche camp to continue talks. They were tasked with overseeing the exchange of an Indian woman and a nine-year-old in return for two Texian prisoners. About an hour later, Damasio and Antonio returned with two redeemed captives: a young girl, Elizabeth Putnam, who had been captured at age two and adopted by a Comanche mother, and a twelve-year-old Mexican child unknown to the Texians. Elizabeth, who could no longer speak English and appeared to have been mistreated, was reunited with her family.

Shortly after, Pivia, a Comanche chief, arrived with two more Texian captives, a boy taken from San Antonio in 1836 and a girl from a ranch near Goliad. Pivia was eager to exchange them for a particular woman held by the Texians. Still, the Texians, recognizing her value, refused, hoping to use her to secure the release of other captives. According to Captain Howard's account, the Comanche still held at least five more captives. In her memoirs, Mary Maverick provided a slightly different version, noting that the woman Pivia sought was the widow of a chief killed in the Council House Fight who owned many mules. She refused to return with Pivia, and the Texians respected her wishes. Instead, Pivia left, dissatisfied, with another Comanche woman, a child, and a blind Indian added to the exchange. Maverick's account, while valuable, may reflect her personal observations and could differ in accuracy from Howard's report.

Before Pivia departed, the Texians and Comanche agreed to send two more representatives to the Comanche camp to select additional prisoners. In return, Pivia would be allowed to choose two more Indian captives, excluding a particular woman the Texians refused to release. Dr. Shields Booker and Cornelius Van Ness, accompanied by Captain Howard and several armed citizens, went to Pivia's camp. They were met by Pivia,

Isamini, and several young warriors, who presented five prisoners while the warriors kept their bows strung, ready for conflict. After tense negotiations lasting nearly an hour, Isamini agreed to release an American boy (Booker Webster's son), a Mexican girl, and one other captive. Maverick noted that Booker's head had been shaved and painted in Indian style, and he reported that the Comanche had killed captives after hearing about the Council House Fight.

After the exchange, Howard continued discussions with Pivia about the remaining captives still held by the Comanche. Pivia, while professing friendship with the Americans, warned that some Comanche factions wanted to fight. Howard made it clear that the Texians were prepared for peace or war, and if the Comanche chose war, they would take the fight directly to their homes.

Pivia remained determined to secure the release of the particular woman he sought and promised to try to buy the remaining American prisoners from other Comanche bands for future exchanges. He also expressed concern that the Penatekas might not have enough captives to trade. Still, Howard assured him that the Texians would accept runaway slaves as part of the exchange to secure the remaining captives.

Following the events involving the Comanche, discipline within the Frontier Regiment in San Antonio began to deteriorate. In May, Pvt. John Robinson of Captain Howard's Company C committed an offense against a female Comanche captive whose husband, a chief, had died in the Council House Fight. As punishment, Colonel Burleson ordered a court martial, leading to Robinson being whipped, his head shaved, and ultimately expelled from the camp after being tarred and feathered on May 20th. The regiment also faced other issues, including a deadly duel, a court-martial, and a mutiny driven by soldiers' frustrations over unpaid wages and unfulfilled promises of land. The mutiny was serious enough to warrant the deployment of Captain Woodhouse's Travis Guards from Austin to restore order. Despite the unrest, loyal soldiers helped suppress the mutiny, leading to the imprisonment of five ringleaders and the execution of two deserters.

The Texians often see the Council House Fight as a significant mistake, but the situation was far more complex. The long-standing tensions between Euroamerican settlers and the Comanche played a major role in the escalating conflict. While the Texians' actions can be criticized in hindsight, the Comanche's inconsistencies and aggression were equally responsible for the deterioration of relations. A violent confrontation between the two groups was likely inevitable, and the Council House Fight was the flashpoint that marked the beginning of the end of Comanche's dominance in Texas.

CHAPTER EIGHT

THE AFTERMATH OF THE COUNCIL HOUSE FIGHT

Immediately after the Council House Fight, the Texas frontier experienced an unusual calm, with no major conflicts or raids between the Texians and the Comanche. Although the Texians anticipated a significant retaliatory attack from the Penateka Comanche, only a few minor skirmishes occurred. The Comanche had lost several key leaders during the fight. Since their leadership was not hereditary, some scholars suggest that it may have taken time for them to reorganize and elect new leaders. However, the quiet was deceptive. In July 1840, a large group of Comanche warriors, possibly numbering up to a thousand, gathered under the leadership of a young chief named Potsanaquahip, also known as Buffalo Hump. This group, accompanied by their families, as well as Kiowa and Mexican guides, prepared for what would become known as the Great Comanche Raid of 1840, one of the boldest and most coordinated Indian attacks in Texas history, which included two of the bloodiest battles ever witnessed in the state.

Anticipating a potential revenge attack for the Council House Fight, Secretary of War Branch T. Archer called for the formation of additional militia companies. However, when weeks passed without significant Comanche retaliation, the volunteers disbanded just before the expected raid occurred. In August, the Comanche moved stealthily south through the settlements, reaching Victoria, Texas, on August 6, 1840. Mistakenly identified as a friendly tribe of Lipans, the Comanche were able to approach the town unnoticed, leading to a surprise attack that resulted in the deaths of several people, including enslaved people working in the fields. They captured over fifteen hundred horses and mules before moving to Linnville, Texas, on August 8.

In Linnville, a major port city, the Comanche surrounded the town, killing two Black men and numerous cattle. They burned and looted stores, warehouses, and homes, forcing the surprised citizens to flee to boats offshore. The Comanche left after plundering the town and capturing more horses, mules, and captives. The raid led to the near-total destruction of Linnville, which never regained its prominence and eventually faded into obscurity, overtaken by the rise of nearby Port Lavaca, Texas.

Several days after the raid on Linnville, on August 12, 1840, Texian forces, including volunteers under Major General Felix Huston and Tonkawan auxiliaries led by Chief Placido, decisively defeated the Comanche at the Battle of Plum Creek. This confrontation featured many notable figures, including Colonel Edward Burleson, Captain Matthew Caldwell, and Texas Rangers led by Ben McCulloch. Following this victory, John H. Moore led an expedition against the Comanche on the upper Colorado River, where his forces killed or captured all the Native Americans they encountered. As a result, the Comanche lost most of the loot from their raids on Victoria and Linnville, including horses, cattle, and mules.

The defeat at Plum Creek had broader implications, frustrating any Mexican plans to use the Comanche as allies in potential campaigns to reclaim Texas, which they had lost in 1836. After the 1840 raid, the Comanche's only significant act of aggression was a raid against Mexicans in the states of Coahuila and Nuevo Leon. Many Texians viewed this raid as evidence of a Mexican-Comanche alliance and as confirmation that the Comanche were frustrated with Mexico's failure to support them during their raids on Victoria and Linnville.

It's likely that the Mexicans significantly influenced the Comanche's decision to target Victoria and Linnville. In late May 1840, Texian officials discovered that General Valentin Canalizo, the Mexican commander in Matamoros, was attempting to incite the Comanche to wage war on the Texians. The

Mexicans had previously engaged with the Cherokee, but by 1840, the Cherokee were no longer present in Texas. Thus, targeting Victoria and Linnville served both the strategic interests of Mexican conspirators and the goals of the Comanche.

General Canalizo's plan to recapture Texas was intricately linked to the resources the Comanche could seize, including thousands of horses and mules, and take from the warehouses in Linnville. Equally crucial was the strategic targeting of Victoria by the Centralist government of Mexico. The Centralists, driven by domestic conflicts with the Federalists, sought to punish Victoria for its role in a previous failed revolution, which had led to the formation of the Republic of the Rio Grande by the Federalist leaders of Tamaulipas, Nuevo Leon, and Coahuila. After suffering a major defeat at the Battle of Santa

Rita de Morelos in March 1840, the revolutionaries took refuge in Texas, setting up their headquarters in Victoria, where they received supplies and recruited volunteers, with much of this support passing through Linnville.

Despite the significant plundering during the Comanche raid, some scholars question the extent of Mexican involvement. The raid was primarily motivated by the Comanche's desire for revenge after the Council House Fight rather than by a conspiracy with Mexico. The Comanche sought to avenge their losses and acquire the weaponry needed to match the Texians' firepower, which drove them to raid Texian stockpiles.

The Council House Fight reshaped the Comanche's relations with their Plains rivals. Due to the economic depression of the late 1830s and the closure of key trading posts, the Comanche struggled to acquire trade goods. To address this, in the summer of 1840, following the Council House Fight, the Penateka Comanche, along with some Kiowa Indians, reached out to the Cheyenne and Arapaho, traditional enemies, to establish peace and gain access to essential trade goods.

The meeting between the Comanche and their new allies, the Cheyenne and Arapaho, at Bent's Fort was significant and well-documented. It began a strategic alliance that had lasting implications for the Southern Plains. The gathering drew considerable attention from the inhabitants of Bent's Fort, who observed the cultural ceremonies that took place over two days. These ceremonies, which included smoking, gift exchanges, and fictive kinship adoptions, were crucial for building trust between the groups. Once they had established a sense of mutual respect and kinship, the Comanche began trading horses for guns, blankets, and other supplies, facilitated by their new allies.

The Cheyenne introduced the Comanche to the Bent brothers, who owned trading posts along the Arkansas River, including Bent's Fort. This introduction opened a new source of munitions and supplies for the Comanche, who began trading with the Bent brothers. In the fall of 1840, the Bent brothers secured a license in St. Louis to trade legally with the Comanche, Kiowa, and Plains Apaches. However, by then, the Comanche had dispersed and headed south with their newly acquired goods.

While the exact extent of Mexican involvement in the Comanche's raid on Texas cities like Victoria and Linnville remains uncertain, Mexico likely played some role in the planning and execution of the raids. Nonetheless, the Comanche's motivations were driven by their desire for revenge and resources to continue their conflict with the Texians. The alliance formed at Bent's Fort marked a significant shift in the power dynamics of the Southern Plains, as it brought together various Indian groups with a common interest in resisting Texian expansion.

The Council House Fight had profound and far-reaching consequences for all parties involved. For the Comanche, losing many of their chiefs was a significant blow, leading to the eventual decline of their power in Texas. The Great Comanche Raid of 1840 was the last major attack on the Republic of Texas by the Comanche. While smaller skirmishes continued, the Texians' success in defending against these raids helped pave the way for westward expansion and settlement.

However, in the short term, the Council House Fight negatively affected the Republic of Texas. The brutal killing of Comanche chiefs during the fight damaged the Republic's reputation abroad. When news of the incident reached Europe, it caused outrage among European leaders, complicating Texas's efforts to secure recognition and foreign loans. General James Hamilton, the Republic's Commissioner in Europe, expressed in a letter to Secretary of State Abner S. Lipscomb that the killings were seen as unforgivable by European diplomats, further straining the Republic's diplomatic efforts at a critical time.

After the tumultuous events of 1840, the future of the Comanche in Texas took a grim turn. The annexation of the Republic of Texas by the United States in 1845 marked the beginning of significant changes in the administration of Indian affairs. With the U.S. Army establishing a line of forts along the frontier by 1849, the protection of Texan citizens became a priority, further constraining the movements and lifestyle of the Comanche.

In 1854, a reservation system was introduced, with a 23,000-acre reservation established on the Clear Fork of the Brazos River for the Penateka Comanche. However, this system was fundamentally at odds with the Comanche's traditional hunter-gatherer way of life. The Penatekas, numbering just over 350 then, struggled with the imposed farming lifestyle, leading many to continue their nomadic existence along the frontier.

The failure of the reservation system in Texas became evident by 1859 when the remaining Comanche were relocated to Indian

Territory near Anadarko, under the jurisdiction of the Wichita Agency. This move marked a significant step towards the eventual decline of the Comanche presence in Texas.

Following the Civil War, the situation for the Comanche worsened with the signing of the Treaty of Medicine Lodge Creek in 1867. This treaty established a reservation in southwestern Indian Territory for the Comanche, Kiowa, and Kiowa-Apache. However, the problems persisted as the Comanche continued to raid Texas from their reservations in Oklahoma.

The escalating tensions culminated in the Red River War of 1874, a decisive campaign by the United States to end the Comanche resistance permanently. This conflict effectively forced the Comanche onto the reservations and marked the end of their dominance on the Texas plains. By the conclusion of the Red River War, the Comanche were confined to the reservations, signaling the final chapter in their struggle to maintain their way of life against the expanding American frontier.

The 1875 United States Reservation Census starkly illustrated the drastic decline of the Comanche population, which had dwindled to just 1,597 individuals. This reduction was coupled with significant cultural disruption as the Comanche were increasingly pressured to abandon their traditional lifestyles as hunters and warriors in favor of farming and stock raising. The reservation system, originally intended to provide security and stability, became a mechanism of further displacement and cultural erosion.

By 1901, the reservation system ended with the distribution of land allotments, promising each Comanche family 160 acres. This policy, however, led to the loss of much of their land and was met with significant protest from the Comanche, who recognized the severe impact it would have on their communal land holdings. Many Comanche, seeking better economic opportunities, left their allotments and moved to urban areas.

Despite these hardships, the Comanche Nation has persevered and adapted over time. Today, the tribe claims an enrolled membership of 13,679 individuals based in Lawton, Oklahoma. The Comanche Nation celebrates and maintains its traditions and history through annual conventions and other cultural events.

The Council House Fight on March 19, 1840, symbolized the broader and often violent interactions between American settlers and the Comanche. This battle culminated in longstanding hostilities and failed negotiations, reflecting the two groups' deep-seated mistrust and cultural misunderstandings. Both the Comanche and the Texians had legitimate reasons for their actions, influenced by a history of conflict and failed diplomacy.

In retrospect, the Council House Fight and its aftermath had significant and long-lasting consequences. The Comanche were gradually stripped of their autonomy and traditional lands. At the same time, the Texians faced diplomatic setbacks as European nations reacted negatively to the violence, complicating their efforts to secure financial support for the Republic. This tumultuous period in Texas history underscores the complex interplay of cultural clashes, resource struggles, and political maneuvers that shaped the early American frontier and its indigenous inhabitants.